DIABETES
COOKBOOK

Appetizing low-sugar, low-fat alternatives to everyday dishes

Fiona Hunter & Heather Whinney

CONTENTS

Guide to symbols

The recipes in this book are accompanied by symbols that alert you to important information.

 Tells you how many people the recipe serves, or how much is produced.

 Indicates how long you will need to prepare and cook a dish. Next to this symbol, it will also state if additional time is required for such things as marinating, standing, proving, or cooling.

 Alerts you to any special preparation or to parts of the recipe that take a long time.

 Denotes that special equipment is required.

 Accompanies freezing information.

  Shows whether a dish is relatively high (3 dots), medium (2 dots), or low (1 dot) on the glycaemic index (GI), and in calories, saturated fat, and salt.

Eating well

Food plays a crucial role in determining our health, vitality, and well-being. Various foods we eat are broken down into glucose, which passes into the bloodstream. Our blood glucose level should not become too high or too low, so to regulate it, the pancreas produces insulin. If you have Type 2 diabetes, you'll know that your pancreas isn't producing enough insulin, or the insulin isn't doing its job properly. (If you have Type 1 diabetes, your body isn't making any insulin at all.)

It is important for everyone to eat healthily, but when you have Type 2 diabetes, diet is even more relevant. Choosing the right foods will help you to manage your condition and reduce the risk of other health problems associated with diabetes. In one study, people with Type 2 diabetes were able to reduce their blood glucose levels by an average of 25 per cent just by following a simple diet plan, similar to the one we recommend. Although people often talk about healthy and unhealthy foods, there is no such thing as a good or a bad food: it is the balance of foods that you eat throughout the day that is important.

HOW THIS BOOK CAN HELP

The recipes in this book are designed to help you achieve a healthy, balanced diet that includes wholegrains, low-GI (glycaemic index) carbohydrates, lean protein, dietary fibre, low-fat dairy products, and plenty of vegetables and fruit. They are also lower in salt, fat and sugar. All this equals a great diet, whether you have Type 2 diabetes or not.

Where the book goes further is in providing "Guidelines per serving" for each recipe (see below), which show you whether a dish is relatively high (3 dots), medium (2 dots) or low (1 dot) in GI (glucose-generating carbohydrates), calories, saturated fat, and salt – the four key dietary areas to watch when you have Type 2 diabetes.

GUIDELINES per serving
- ●●○   **GI**
- ●●●   **calories**
- ●○○   **saturated fat**
- ●●○   **salt**

A healthy shopping basket

It's very easy to opt for convenience rather than nutritional quality, so take some time to review the contents of your shopping trolley. Making small changes – such as switching from full-fat to semi-skimmed milk, and from white to wholemeal bread – can make a real difference to your health, and help you to manage diabetes.

BE A SAVVY SHOPPER

1 Walk around the perimeter of the store first: the fresh foods are usually there. Approach central aisles with caution: highly processed foods lurk here.
2 Compare brands of processed food to find which has least fat, salt, and sugar, and the most fibre. Look at the figures per 100g rather than per serving.
3 Choose fresh and minimally processed foods, such as 100 per cent fruit juice or all-wholegrain items.
4 Try to avoid foods with added salt or sugar; if necessary, you can add it sparingly yourself.
5 Look at ingredients – the longer the list of additives, the less healthy a food usually is.
6 Don't forget frozen vegetables – they save you time because they are already prepared, and they often contain more vitamins than fresh vegetables.

FRUIT AND VEGETABLES
Eat from a wide range of fruit and vegetables for different vitamins, minerals, and phytochemicals Fresh, frozen, canned, and dried varieties all count towards your five a day.

OIL
Use unsaturated oils such as olive, rapeseed, walnut, avocado, linseed (flaxseed), and soya bean for omega-6 and omega-3 fats.

EGGS

If you don't eat oil-rich fish, choose eggs that advertise themselves as especially rich in omega-3 fats. Eggs are also a good source of iron.

BREAKFAST CEREALS

Choose wholegrain breakfast cereals without added sugar, with at least 3g fibre per serving. Alternatively, make muesli from oats, seeds, nuts, and dried fruit.

DAIRY PRODUCTS

You can obtain a good supply of protein and calcium from dairy products; go for low-fat versions if possible.

RICE

Choose basmati or brown rice, which has a lower GI than long-grain white rice and is a good source of B-vitamins.

OIL-RICH FISH

Oil-rich fish such as mackerel, salmon, and fresh tuna provide omega-3 fats, which help heart health. Eat at least one portion a week; choose a different type of fish for another meal during the week.

POULTRY AND LEAN MEAT

Choose chicken and lean meat rather than fatty cuts of meat. Keep portions modest – 100–140g (3½–5oz) is more than enough for one person.

CANNED BEANS

Beans are high in fibre and have a low GI. Look for the ones canned without salt or sugar; if canned in brine, rinse thoroughly before using.

BREAD

Buy wholegrain bread. It is more nutritious than white and has a lower GI.

Rainbow muesli

This is a wonderfully satisfying muesli mix, which will sustain your energy levels throughout the morning. A great breakfast to have on standby in the storecupboard.

INGREDIENTS

100g (3½oz) rye flakes
100g (3½oz) barley flakes
100g (3½oz) porridge oats
100g (3½oz) golden raisins
100g (3½oz) ready-to-eat dried
  apricots, roughly chopped
50g (1¾oz) hazelnuts,
  roughly chopped
50g (1¾oz) pumpkin seeds
50g (1¾oz) sunflower seeds

METHOD

1 Mix together all the dry ingredients in a bowl and transfer to an airtight container until needed (there are 13 servings).
2 Serve with chilled semi-skimmed milk or a little plain reduced-fat yogurt. For a delicious treat, you could add some seasonal fresh fruit such as blueberries or raspberries.

makes 650g
13 servings

prep 10 mins

GUIDELINES per serving

● ○ ○ GI
● ○ ○ calories
● ○ ○ saturated fat
● ○ ○ salt

Breakfast smoothie

Smoothies are a great way to boost your intake of fruit, and this sustaining recipe will give you a shot of calcium as well as vitamins and minerals.

INGREDIENTS
2 small, ripe bananas
500ml (16fl oz) semi-skimmed milk
3 tbsp oatmeal
100g (3½oz) fresh raspberries
150ml (7fl oz) fat-free Greek yogurt
1/2 tsp ground cinnamon

METHOD
1 Cut the bananas into small chunks and place in a blender along with the remaining ingredients. Blend at high speed for 1–2 minutes or until smooth.
2 Pour into two glasses and drink immediately.

serves 2

prep 5 mins

GUIDELINES per serving

GI

calories

saturated fat

salt

Apple and oat pancakes

These little pancakes are a perfect treat for the weekend. The oats used in the mixture provide soluble fibre and help to slow down the absorption of carbohydrate.

INGREDIENTS
125g (4½oz) plain flour
1 tsp baking powder
75g (2½oz) porridge oats
2–3 tbsp caster sugar
pinch of ground cinnamon
2 eggs, separated
284ml carton buttermilk
2 medium apples
sunflower oil, for frying

METHOD
1 Sift the flour into a large bowl and mix with the baking powder. Stir in the oats, sugar, and cinnamon. Make a well in the centre and beat in the egg yolks and buttermilk to make a thick batter (it should have the consistency of heavy cream).

2 Core the apples, coarsely grate the flesh, and stir into the batter mixture. Whisk the egg whites until stiff but not dry and fold into the batter.

3 Heat a griddle pan or large heavy-based non-stick frying pan over a moderate heat. Add a tiny drop of oil to the hot pan. When the pan is hot, drop a heaped dessertspoon of the batter into the pan and flatten slightly with the back of the spoon, so that the pancakes are about 10cm (4in) in diameter and about 5mm (¼in) thick.

4 Cook for 2 minutes or until bubbles start to break on the surface and the pancakes are firm enough to flip. Flip and cook for 1–2 minutes more, until they feel springy when prodded. Transfer to a warm oven while you cook the rest, adding more oil as necessary. Try with fresh summer fruits and low-fat Greek yogurt, or your own favourite topping.

makes 12
serves 4–6

prep 10 mins
• cook 15 mins

GUIDELINES per serving

GI

calories

saturated fat

salt

Tomato and bean soup

A flavoursome Mediterranean-style soup.

INGREDIENTS

1 tbsp olive oil
1 onion, finely chopped
salt and freshly ground
  black pepper
2 garlic cloves, finely chopped
1 tsp fennel seeds
6 tomatoes, skinned and quartered
1 tbsp tomato purée
400g can of chopped tomatoes
400g can of borlotti beans,
  drained and rinsed
400g can of cannellini beans,
  drained and rinsed
500ml (16fl oz) vegetable stock
chopped parsley, to serve

METHOD

1 Heat the olive oil in a large pan, add the onion, and cook over a low heat for 7–8 minutes until it softens and turns transparent. Season with a pinch of salt and some black pepper. Stir in the garlic and the fennel seeds.

2 Add the fresh tomatoes and break them up with the back of a spoon. Stir in the tomato purée and canned tomatoes.

3 Tip in the beans, add the stock and bring to the boil. Reduce the heat to a simmer and cook, uncovered, for about 20 minutes, topping up with more stock if needed. Taste and season as necessary. Stir through a little chopped parsley and serve.

serves 4

prep 10 mins
• cook 20 mins

GUIDELINES per serving

GI

calories

saturated fat

salt

Chicken broth with herby dumplings

A substantial broth for cold, rainy nights when you want to treat yourself to some comfort food.

INGREDIENTS

900ml (1½ pints) chicken stock, plus 500ml (16fl oz) extra

2 skinless chicken breasts

200g (7oz) baby button mushrooms, any larger ones halved

50g (1¾oz) flat-leaf parsley, finely chopped

salt and freshly ground black pepper

15g (½oz) fresh Parmesan, grated, to serve

For the dumplings

100g (3½oz) vegetable suet

6 sage leaves, finely chopped

50g (1¾oz) fresh thyme leaves

175g (6oz) fresh white breadcrumbs

3 eggs

METHOD

1 First, make the broth. Pour 900ml (1½ pints) chicken stock into a large pan and bring to the boil. Add the chicken, reduce the heat until the stock is simmering, partially cover the pan, and cook for about 20 minutes or until the chicken is done. Remove the chicken with a slotted spoon and set aside.

2 While the chicken is cooking, prepare the dumplings. Tip the suet, herbs, breadcrumbs, and eggs into a bowl, season, and mix well. Form into a dough – add a little water if necessary to get the dough to start clinging together in lumps. Shape into balls the size of a walnut, and put on a plate.

3 Top up the broth with the remaining stock, bring to the boil, part-cover, and simmer for 10 minutes. Add the dumplings and mushrooms and poach for 10 minutes. Slice or tear the chicken and return it to pan with the parsley. Heat through. Season and serve sprinkled with a little Parmesan.

serves 4

prep 5 mins
• cook 45 mins

3 months

GUIDELINES per serving

GI

calories

saturated fat

salt

13

Carrot and ginger soup

Unlike most vegetables, which are most nutritious when eaten raw, cooking carrots increases the availability of betacarotene, which the body can convert into vitamin A.

INGREDIENTS

2 tbsp olive oil
1 large onion, peeled and
   finely chopped
1 clove of garlic, peeled and crushed
5cm (2in) piece of fresh root ginger,
   peeled and finely chopped
600g (1lb 5oz) carrots, peeled
   and roughly chopped
750ml (1¼ pints) vegetable stock
zest and juice of 2 large oranges
salt and freshly ground black pepper
spring onions, chopped, to garnish

METHOD

1 Heat the oil in large non-stick saucepan, add the onion and cook over a medium heat for 3–4 minutes. Add the garlic, ginger, and carrots and continue to cook for a further 5 minutes, stirring occasionally.

2 Add the stock, orange zest and juice, and season to taste with salt and black pepper. Bring to the boil, then reduce the heat, cover, and simmer for 40 minutes or until the carrots are soft.

3 Transfer the soup to a food processor or blender and process until smooth, then return to the pan and reheat gently. If the soup is too thick, you can thin it out with a little extra stock or water. Ladle the soup into bowls, garnish with chopped spring onions, and serve.

serves 4

prep 15 mins
• cook 50 mins

3 months

food processor

GUIDELINES per serving

●●○○	GI
●○○○	calories
●○○○	saturated fat
●●○○	salt

Falafel

Based on chickpeas, these tasty and substantial bites are a Middle Eastern classic.

INGREDIENTS

225g (8oz) dried chickpeas, soaked
   overnight in cold water
1 tbsp tahini
1 garlic clove, crushed
1 tsp salt
1 tsp ground cumin
1 tsp turmeric
1 tsp ground coriander
½ tsp cayenne pepper
2 tbsp finely chopped parsley
juice of 1 small lemon
vegetable oil, for frying

METHOD

1 Drain the soaked chickpeas and place them in a food processor with the rest of the ingredients. Process until finely chopped but not puréed.
2 Transfer the mixture to a bowl and set it aside for at least 30 minutes (and up to 8 hours), covered in the refrigerator.
3 Wet your hands and shape the mixture into 12 balls. Press the tops down slightly to flatten.
4 Heat 5cm (2in) of oil in a deep pan or wok. Fry the balls in batches for 3–4 minutes, or until lightly golden. Drain on kitchen paper and serve. A simple green salad makes a good accompaniment.

serves 4

prep 25 mins plus soaking and chilling • cook 15 mins

food processor

GUIDELINES per serving

 GI

 calories

saturated fat

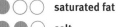 salt

Tortilla

This variation of a traditional thick Spanish omelette includes broccoli and peas as well as potatoes.

INGREDIENTS

115g (4oz) fresh or frozen peas
115g (4oz) broccoli florets
4 tbsp olive oil
350g (12oz) floury potatoes, such as
  King Edward, peeled and cut into
  2cm (¾in) cubes

2 small red onions, finely chopped
6 eggs, beaten
salt and freshly ground
  black pepper

METHOD

1 Bring a large saucepan of lightly salted water to the boil over a high heat. Add the peas and boil for 5 minutes, or until just tender. Use a slotted spoon to transfer the peas to a bowl of cold water. Return the pan to the boil, add the broccoli and boil for 4 minutes or until just tender. Remove the florets and add to the peas to cool, then drain both vegetables well, and set aside.

2 Heat 3 tablespoons oil in a non-stick frying pan over a medium heat. Add the potatoes and onions, and cook for 10–15 minutes, stirring often, or until the potatoes are tender.

3 Beat the eggs in a large bowl, and season with salt and pepper, then use a slotted spoon to transfer the potatoes and onions to the eggs. Add the peas and broccoli and gently stir. Discard excess oil from the pan, plus any crispy bits stuck to the bottom.

4 Heat the remaining oil in the pan over a high heat. Add the egg mixture, immediately reduce the heat to low, and smooth the surface. Leave to cook for 20–25 minutes, or until the top of the omelette begins to set and the base is golden brown.

5 Carefully slide the tortilla on to a plate, place a second plate on top and invert so that the cooked side is on top. Slide the tortilla back into the pan and cook for 5 minutes, until both sides are golden brown and set. Remove from the heat and leave to set for at least 5 minutes. Serve warm or cooled, cut into wedges.

serves 4

**prep 15 mins
• cook 45 mins**

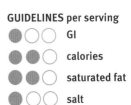

GUIDELINES per serving
GI
calories
saturated fat
salt

17

Lentil loaf

Lentils are a good source of protein and iron, and this substantial loaf can be eaten hot or cold.

INGREDIENTS

175g (6oz) red lentils
450ml (15fl oz) vegetable stock
1 tbsp olive oil
1 onion, sliced
2 sticks celery, finely chopped
1 red pepper, deseeded and diced
1 clove garlic, crushed
1 small red chilli, deseeded and
  finely chopped

125g (4½oz) shiitake mushrooms,
  finely chopped
150g (5½oz) half-fat Cheddar
  cheese, grated
225g (8oz) wholemeal breadcrumbs
3 tbsp chopped fresh coriander
1 egg, beaten
salt and freshly ground black pepper

METHOD

1 Put the lentils in a saucepan and add the stock. Bring to the boil, then reduce the heat, cover and simmer over a low heat for 15–20 minutes or until the lentils are very soft.

2 Preheat the oven to 180°C (350°F/Gas 4). Grease and line the bottom of a 1.2 litre (2 pint) loaf tin. Heat the oil in a frying pan, add the onion and cook for 2–3 minutes or until softened. Add the celery, red pepper, garlic, chilli, and mushrooms. Cook, stirring, for 10 minutes.

3 Tip the vegetables into the lentil mixture, then stir in the cheese, breadcrumbs, coriander, and egg. Mix well and season to taste with salt and pepper.

4 Spoon the mixture into the prepared loaf tin and bake for 1 hour or until firm to the touch.

5 Cool in the tin for 10 minutes before turning out. Cut into thick slices and serve hot or cold.

serves 6

prep 15 mins
• cook 1 hour 20 mins

GUIDELINES per serving

GI
calories
saturated fat
salt

Vegetable chop suey

A super-quick dish that makes a perfect midweek supper.

INGREDIENTS

2 tbsp vegetable oil
1 onion, finely chopped
2 carrots, finely sliced
200g (7oz) baby corn
200g (7oz) mangetout
3 garlic cloves, finely chopped
200g can bamboo shoots, drained
200g (7oz) oyster mushrooms,
   large ones halved
400g (14oz) beansprouts
bunch of spring onions, trimmed
   and sliced
1 tbsp dark soy sauce
splash of sesame oil
freshly ground black pepper
15g (½oz) dry-roasted peanuts,
   chopped

METHOD

1 Heat the oil in a wok and when just starting to smoke, add the onion and carrots and stir-fry for a few minutes. Then add the baby corn and mangetout and stir-fry for 1 minute.

2 Add the garlic, bamboo shoots, mushrooms, beansprouts, and spring onions, and stir-fry for another minute or two. Keep everything moving all the time.

3 Add the soy sauce and sesame oil and season with black pepper. Stir-fry for 1 minute and then tip out the vegetables onto a serving dish, top with the peanuts and serve.

serves 4

prep 15 mins
• cook 5 mins

wok

GUIDELINES per serving

● ○ ○ GI
● ○ ○ calories
● ○ ○ saturated fat
● ● ○ salt

Chicken tostada with avocado salsa

A tasty and filling lunch or supper dish that is full of flavour and high in dietary fibre.

INGREDIENTS

6 tomatoes, skinned, quartered, and seeds removed

1 large red onion, peeled and sliced into thin wedges

1 small red pepper, deseeded and roughly chopped

3 cloves of garlic, unpeeled

1 red chilli, deseeded

3 tbsp olive oil

salt and freshly ground black pepper

415g can mixed beans, rinsed and drained

400g (14oz) cooked chicken, shredded

8 wholemeal flour tortillas

For the salsa

6 tomatoes, seeds removed and flesh diced

2 small ripe avocado, peeled, stones removed, and flesh diced

1 small red onion, finely chopped

3 tbsp chopped fresh coriander

juice of 1 lime

METHOD

1 Preheat the oven to 200°C (400°F/Gas 6). Place the tomatoes, onions, red pepper, garlic, and chilli in a roasting tin, drizzle with oil, and bake for 20–30 minutes or until soft and slightly charred. Squeeze the garlic cloves from their skins and place in a food processor along with the other cooked vegetables and process until smooth. Season to taste with salt and black pepper.

2 Place the beans in a large saucepan and cook over a low heat for 2 minutes. Add the vegetable sauce, stir in the chicken, and cook for a further 2 minutes, stirring occasionally.

3 To make the salsa, mix all the ingredients together in a bowl, and season to taste.

4 Heat the tortillas according to the packet instructions. To serve, spoon a little of the chicken mixture into each tortilla, fold, and serve with the salsa.

serves 4

prep 15 mins
• cook 50 mins

food processor

GUIDELINES per serving

GI

calories

saturated fat

salt

Spaghetti with tomatoes and goat's cheese

Fresh cherry tomatoes are the basis for an instant cheesy topping that doesn't need cooking: just heap it on plates of steaming spaghetti.

INGREDIENTS

20 cherry tomatoes, halved
1 tbsp capers, rinsed and dried
3 tbsp fruity extra virgin olive oil
2 garlic cloves, finely chopped
150g (5½oz) semi-hard goat's
   cheese, broken or sliced into chunks
1 tsp dried oregano
1 tbsp fresh basil, chopped
salt and freshly ground
   black pepper
350g (12oz) spaghetti

METHOD

1 Put all the ingredients except for the spaghetti in a bowl. Season well with salt and black pepper, and set aside for about 20 minutes for the flavours to mingle and develop.
2 When ready to serve, cook the spaghetti in a pan of salted boiling water for 8–10 minutes or according to the instructions on the packet. Drain, then return to the pan with a little of the cooking water.
3 Add the tomato mixture to the spaghetti and toss well to coat. Serve immediately.

serves 4

**prep 10 mins
plus standing
• cook 10 mins**

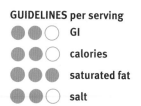

GUIDELINES per serving

●●○ GI

●●○ calories

●●● saturated fat

●●○ salt

Mushroom lasagne

A meatless lasagne made with robust mushrooms and flavour-packed leeks.

INGREDIENTS

1 tbsp olive oil

2 leeks, trimmed and finely chopped

400g (14oz) white and chestnut mushrooms, half of them chopped, half grated

3 garlic cloves, finely chopped

1 tbsp plain flour

300ml (10fl oz) semi-skimmed milk

salt and freshly ground black pepper

pinch of dried oregano

100g (3½oz) fresh Parmesan cheese, grated

6 tomatoes, deseeded and diced

10 lasagne sheets (no need for precooked ones)

METHOD

1 Preheat the oven to 200°C (400°F/Gas 6). Heat the olive oil in a large pan, add the leeks and cook for 5–8 minutes until soft. Add all the mushrooms plus the garlic, and cook for a further 5–8 minutes until the mushrooms begin to release their juices.

2 Stir in the flour and combine it well with the juices in the pan. Remove from the heat, add a little of the milk and stir until smooth. Return to the heat and add the remaining milk, little by little, until you have a smooth sauce. Season well with salt and black pepper, then add the oregano and Parmesan. Stir in the tomatoes.

3 Coat the bottom of an ovenproof baking dish with some of the sauce, then a layer of lasagne; continue adding alternate layers, ending with some sauce as the topping. Put the dish in the oven to bake for 15–20 minutes, or until the sauce is golden and bubbling.

serves 4

prep 20 mins
• cook 45 mins

3 months

GUIDELINES per serving

●●○ GI

●●○ calories

●●○ saturated fat

●○○ salt

Brown rice, red pepper and artichoke risotto

Not a risotto in the true sense, but a great mix of flavours and textures.

INGREDIENTS

1 tbsp olive oil
1 onion, finely chopped
salt and freshly ground black pepper
2 sweet pointed red peppers,
   halved, deseeded and chopped
pinch of chilli flakes
280g (10oz) brown rice
1 litre (1¾ pints) vegetable stock
280g jar of artichoke hearts,
   drained and roughly chopped
handful of flat-leaf parsley,
   finely chopped

METHOD

1 Heat the oil in a large frying pan then add the onion and cook on a low heat until soft and transparent. Season with a pinch of salt and some freshly ground black pepper. Add the red peppers and cook for a few minutes until they soften.

2 Add the chilli flakes, then stir in the rice. Raise the heat a little, pour in a ladleful of the stock, and bring to the boil. Reduce to a simmer and cook gently for 40–50 minutes, adding a little more stock each time the liquid is absorbed, until the rice is cooked.

3 Stir through the artichokes and cook for a couple of minutes to heat through, then taste and season as required. Cover with a lid, remove from the heat and leave for 10 minutes, then stir through the chopped parsley and transfer to plates or bowls. You could serve this with a rocket salad on the side.

serves 4

prep 10 mins
• cook 50 mins - 1 hour

GUIDELINES per serving

GI

calories

saturated fat

salt

Leek and tomato pilaf

This version of a pilaf uses pearl barley instead of rice.

INGREDIENTS
2 tbsp olive oil
1 large leek, trimmed and
　roughly chopped
85g (3oz) pearl barley, rinsed
400g can chopped tomatoes
1 tbsp tomato purée
pinch of smoked paprika
500ml (16fl oz) vegetable stock
150g (5½oz) frozen soya beans
pinch of chilli flakes
salt and freshly ground black pepper
15g (½oz) Parmesan cheese
　shavings, to serve

METHOD
1　Heat the oil in a large, deep frying pan, put the leek in and fry it for 2–3 minutes. Stir in the pearl barley and cook for a further minute.
2　Add the tomatoes, tomato purée, paprika, and 400ml (14fl oz) of the stock. Cover and simmer for 20 minutes, stirring occasionally and adding more stock as it is absorbed.
3　Stir in the soya beans and chilli flakes, and season to taste with salt and pepper. Cook for a further 5 minutes or until the barley is soft and the soya beans are heated through. Serve immediately, sprinkled with Parmesan shavings.

serves 2

prep 5 mins
• cook 30 mins

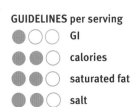

GUIDELINES per serving
●○○○　GI
●●○○　calories
●●○○　saturated fat
●●○○　salt

Chorizo, chickpea, and mango salad

A hearty, main meal salad with great variety of flavour.

INGREDIENTS
1 tbsp olive oil
150g (5½oz) chorizo, roughly chopped
400g can of chickpeas,
   drained and rinsed
3 cloves of garlic, finely chopped
handful of flat-leaf parsley,
   finely chopped
1 tbsp dry sherry
2 ripe mangos, stoned,
   and flesh diced
small handful of fresh basil,
   roughly chopped
small handful of fresh mint leaves,
   roughly chopped
small handful of fresh coriander leaves,
   roughly chopped
250g (9oz) baby spinach leaves

METHOD
1 Heat the olive oil in a frying pan, add the chorizo and chickpeas and cook over a low heat for 1 minute, then add the garlic and parsley and cook for a further minute. Add the sherry and cook for 10 minutes, stirring occasionally.
2 Put the mango and remaining herbs in a bowl and toss together, then add the chickpea mixture and combine well. Spoon onto a bed of spinach to serve.

serves 2

prep 15 mins
• cook 15 mins

GUIDELINES per serving
● ● ○ GI
● ● ● calories
● ● ● saturated fat
● ● ○ salt

Vermicelli noodles with prawns and crab

A light, quick, Asian-style dish full of aromatic flavours, prepared in a wok.

INGREDIENTS

5cm (2in) piece of fresh root ginger, roughly chopped

2 tsp Sichuan pepper

3 garlic cloves

1 stalk lemongrass, trimmed and woody outer leaf removed

salt and freshly ground black pepper

2 tbsp sunflower oil

250g (9oz) peeled prawns, raw

¼ small pumpkin or butternut squash (about 140g/5oz), grated

200g (7oz) fresh white crabmeat

1 tbsp rice vinegar

400ml (14fl oz) vegetable or chicken stock

225g (8oz) vermicelli noodles

1 bunch of spring onions, finely chopped, to garnish

METHOD

1 Put the ginger, Sichuan pepper, garlic, and lemongrass in a food processor or blender and whiz until chopped. Season with salt and black pepper and whiz again. Heat 1 tablespoon of oil in a wok, swirling it around to coat. When the oil is hot, add the prawns and cook until pink (2–4 minutes). Remove and set aside.

2 Pour the remaining oil into the wok, add the ginger mixture to the pan and stir for a couple of minutes. Add the grated pumpkin and cook for a further 5 minutes, until the pumpkin has softened. Stir in the crabmeat.

3 Add the rice vinegar and the stock, and bring to the boil. Toss in the vermicelli noodles and stir for 5–8 minutes until the clump breaks down and the noodles begin to soften. Stir the cooked prawns into the mixture. Taste, season if needed, and then sprinkle with the spring onions to serve.

serves 4

prep 10 mins
• cook 20 mins

food processor
and wok

GUIDELINES per serving

●●○ GI

●●○ calories

●○○ saturated fat

●●○ salt

Tuna with black-eyed bean and avocado salsa

Serving fish or meat with a spicy salsa like this one is a great way to add to your intake of fruit and vegetables.

INGREDIENTS

400g can black-eyed beans,
   rinsed and drained
2 ripe avocados, peeled, stoned,
   and diced
200g (7oz) plum tomatoes, cut into
   quarters, deseeded and diced
1 small red onion, finely chopped
4 tbsp chopped fresh coriander
zest and juice of 2 limes
salt and freshly ground black pepper
4 fresh tuna steaks (about
   150g/5½oz each)
1 tbsp olive oil

METHOD

1 To make the salsa, mix together the beans, avocados, tomatoes, and onion
   in a large bowl. Stir in the coriander, lime zest and juice, and season to taste.
2 Brush the tuna steaks with oil. Place on a hot griddle pan and sear for
   4–5 minutes each side.
3 Transfer the tuna to a warm serving plate and serve with the salsa.

serves 4

prep 10 mins
• cook 15 mins

GUIDELINES per serving

GI

calories

saturated fat

salt

Spicy mackerel and beetroot roast

Mackerel, an oily fish that is rich in essential fatty acids, marries well with sweet beetroot and Indian spices.

INGREDIENTS

4 whole fresh mackerel, cleaned, gutted, and slashed
300g (10oz) cooked beetroot
1 tbsp olive oil
1 tbsp fresh coriander leaves, to garnish

1 red chilli, deseeded and chopped
½ tbsp sherry vinegar or red wine vinegar
1 tbsp olive oil
salt and freshly ground black pepper

For the spice rub

1 tsp cumin seeds
1 tsp coriander seeds
2 garlic cloves, roughly chopped

METHOD

1 Preheat the oven to 200°C (400°F/Gas 6). First, make the spice rub. Put all the ingredients in a food processor or blender and whiz until ground. Alternatively, grind in a pestle and mortar.

2 Rub the paste all over the fish and into the slashes. Put the beetroot in a roasting tin and toss in 1 tablespoon of oil. Add the fish and place in the oven for 8–10 minutes or until cooked and crispy. Sprinkle with the coriander leaves to serve. You could accompany this with a little brown or basmati rice.

makes 4

prep 15 mins
• cook 10 mins

food processor

GUIDELINES per serving
GI
calories
saturated fat
salt

Chicken and artichoke filo pie

Filo pastry is quick and easy to use and a healthier alternative to shortcrust or flaky pastry, as it contains considerably less fat.

INGREDIENTS

3 tbsp vegetable oil
1 large onion, finely chopped
4 skinless chicken breasts, cut into bite-sized chunks
1 clove garlic, crushed
4 sticks celery, chopped
200g (7oz) low-fat soft cheese with garlic and herbs

400g can artichokes, drained and roughly chopped
salt and freshly ground black pepper
6 large sheets of filo pastry
1 tsp sesame seeds

METHOD

1 Preheat the oven to 190°C (375°F/Gas 5). Heat 2 tablespoons of the oil in a large frying pan and add the onion. Cook, stirring, for 2–3 minutes or until soft. Add the chicken, garlic, and celery and cook for 5 minutes or until the chicken is golden brown all over.

2 Remove from the heat, stir in the soft cheese and artichokes, and season to taste. Transfer the mixture into a shallow ovenproof dish.

3 Lightly brush the sheets of filo pastry with the remaining oil, then scrunch each sheet slightly and place it on top of the chicken mixture. Sprinkle with sesame seeds and bake in the oven for 20–25 minutes or until the pastry is crisp and golden. Serve hot.

serves 4

prep 15 mins
• cook 25-30 mins

GUIDELINES per serving

GI

calories

saturated fat

salt

Chicken nuggets

Tender bites of moist chicken in a golden coating.

INGREDIENTS

4 slices of white bread
1 tsp paprika
salt and freshly ground black pepper
1–2 eggs, lightly beaten
plain flour, for dusting
2 skinless chicken breasts,
  cut into strips
olive oil, for oiling

METHOD

1 Preheat the oven to 200°C (400°F/Gas 6). Place the bread in a food processor and whiz to crumbs, then sprinkle in the paprika, a pinch of salt and some black pepper and whiz again. Tip the crumbs onto a baking sheet, spread them out evenly then bake for 3–6 minutes until golden, giving them a gentle stir halfway through.

2 Return the toasted crumbs to the food processor and whiz again until fine. Tip out onto a large plate.

3 Pour the beaten egg onto another large plate and tip the flour onto a third large plate. Toss the chicken pieces in the egg first, then coat them with the flour and finally the breadcrumbs. Oil a baking sheet well with olive oil and sit the coated chicken pieces on it. Bake in the oven for 15–20 minutes or until the chicken is cooked and the coating is golden.

serves 4

prep 20 mins
• cook 20 mins

1 month

food processor

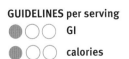

GUIDELINES per serving

GI

calories

saturated fat

salt

Chicken and apricot tagine

The dried fruit and warm spices in this dish are the unmistakable flavours of the Middle East.

INGREDIENTS

2 tbsp sunflower oil
1 onion, finely chopped
1 garlic clove, finely chopped
1 tsp ground ginger
1 tsp ground cumin
1 tsp turmeric
pinch of ground cinnamon
pinch of dried chilli flakes
1 tbsp tomato purée

600ml (1 pint) chicken stock
4 tbsp fresh orange juice
150g (5½oz) mixed dried fruit, such
  as apricots and raisins
salt and freshly ground black pepper
675g (1½lb) skinless boneless chicken
  breasts and thighs, cut into large chunks
2 tbsp chopped fresh coriander, to garnish

METHOD

1 Heat the oil in a large flameproof casserole over a medium heat. Add the onion, garlic, ground spices, and chilli flakes and fry, stirring, for 5 minutes, or until the onions have softened. Stir in the tomato purée and stock and bring to the boil, stirring.

2 Add the orange juice, dried fruits, and salt and pepper to taste. Reduce the heat, partially cover the pan, and simmer for 15 minutes, or until the fruits are soft and the juices have reduced slightly.

3 Add the chicken, re-cover the casserole, and continue simmering for 20 minutes, or until the chicken is tender and the juices run clear. Adjust the seasoning, if necessary, then garnish with coriander and serve hot.

serves 4

prep 15 mins
• cook 35-45 mins

GUIDELINES per serving
GI
calories
saturated fat
salt

Quick turkey cassoulet

A hearty, filling supper dish that is high in fibre.

INGREDIENTS

3 tbsp olive oil

1 medium red onion, peeled
and finely chopped

2 cloves of garlic, peeled and crushed

1 red pepper, deseeded and diced

60g (2oz) smoked back bacon,
roughly chopped

2 celery stalks, finely chopped

400g can of chopped tomatoes

250ml (8fl oz) chicken stock

2 tsp dark soy sauce

75g (2½oz) wholemeal breadcrumbs

50g (1¾oz) freshly grated
Parmesan cheese

3 tbsp chopped flat-leaf parsley

2 tsp Dijon mustard

2 x 400g cans of mixed beans,
rinsed and drained

400g (14oz) cooked turkey
breast, roughly chopped

METHOD

1 Heat 2 tablespoons of the oil in a large saucepan, add the onion, and cook over a
   low heat for 5 minutes. Add the garlic, red pepper, bacon, and celery and cook for
   a further 5 minutes, stirring occasionally.

2 Add the tomatoes, stock, and soy sauce. Bring to the boil, then reduce to a fast
   simmer and cook for 15 minutes or until the sauce begins to thicken.

3 Meanwhile, mix together the breadcrumbs, Parmesan, and parsley. Set aside.

4 Add the mustard, beans, and turkey to the saucepan and cook for a further
   5 minutes until heated through.

5 Transfer the hot mixture to a shallow ovenproof dish. Sprinkle the breadcrumb
   mixture evenly over the top and drizzle over the remaining olive oil. Place
   under a medium-hot grill for 5 minutes or until the top is golden brown. Serve
   immediately.

serves 6

prep 15 mins
• cook 35 mins

GUIDELINES per serving

GI

calories

saturated fat

salt

Cajun chicken with sweetcorn salsa

Avocados give the salsa a wonderfully creamy flavour, which helps to balance the fieriness of the chicken.

INGREDIENTS

2 skinless chicken breasts
1 tbsp of Cajun seasoning
1 tbsp olive oil

For the salsa

1 large fresh corn on the cob,
  stripped of husks and threads

½ small red onion, finely chopped
½ red pepper, deseeded and diced
1 red chilli, deseeded and
  finely chopped
1 small hass avocado, diced
1 tbsp olive oil
juice of 1 lime

METHOD

1 Put the chicken breasts between 2 pieces of cling film and pound with a rolling pin until flattened evenly. Mix the the Cajun seasoning with the oil and brush over the flattened chicken. Leave to marinate for at least 15 minutes.

2 To make the salsa, add the corn to a large pan of boiling water and cook for 5 minutes, then immediately transfer to a bowl of iced water to cool. Drain well, then, using a sharp knife, scrape off all the kernels. Combine with the remaining salsa ingredients, mix well, and set aside.

3 Heat a griddle pan and cook the chicken for 4–5 minutes on one side, pressing the pieces down on the griddle pan, then turn and cook for 4–5 minutes on the other side, or until cooked through.

4 Spoon the salsa onto serving plates and top with the griddled chicken.

serves 2

prep 10 mins
• cook 15 mins

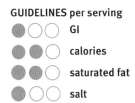

GUIDELINES per serving

GI

calories

saturated fat

salt

Spicy cottage pie with lentils

In this recipe, some of the meat has been replaced with lentils to reduce the fat content of the dish and boost fibre.

INGREDIENTS

2 tbsp olive oil
400g (14oz) extra-lean minced beef
1 large onion, finely chopped
3 sticks celery, finely chopped
2 garlic cloves, crushed
1 red pepper, deseeded and diced
2 tbsp plain flour
½ tsp ground cinnamon
2 tbsp tomato purée
150ml (5fl oz) red wine
1 tsp dried thyme
300–400ml (10–14fl oz) beef stock
1 tsp Worcestershire sauce

pinch of dried chilli flakes
400g can lentils, rinsed and drained

For the mash

450g (1lb) white potatoes, peeled and cut
  into even-sized chunks
600g (1lb 5oz) sweet potatoes, peeled
  and cut into even-sized chunks
150ml (5fl oz) hot semi-skimmed milk
25g (scant 1oz) polyunsaturated margarine
salt and freshly ground black pepper
1 tbsp sunflower or pumpkin seeds

METHOD

1 Preheat the oven to 200°C (400°F/Gas 6). Heat 1 tablespoon of oil in a frying pan. Brown mince over a high heat for 1–2 minutes; set aside. Add remaining oil to the pan and cook onion over a medium heat for 2 minutes. Add the celery, garlic, and red pepper. Cook for 2 minutes. Return meat to the pan. Add flour, cinnamon, tomato purée, and wine. Cook, stirring, for 1 minute. Add the thyme, 300ml (10fl oz) stock, the Worcestershire sauce, and chilli flakes. Season to taste. Bring to the boil, reduce the heat, cover and simmer for 30 minutes, adding more stock if needed. Take off the heat and stir in the lentils.

2 Boil the potatoes and sweet potatoes for 15–20 minutes, or until tender. Drain, then return to the pan. Add the milk and margarine, and mash well. Season to taste. Spoon tmeat mixture into an ovenproof dish, spread the mash on top, and sprinkle with the seeds. Place pie on a baking tray and cook in the oven for 20–25 minutes.

serves 4

prep 20 mins
• cook 1 hour

3 months

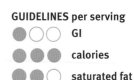
GUIDELINES per serving
GI
calories
saturated fat
salt

Lamb cutlets with chermoula

Chermoula is a classic Moroccan spice marinade, wonderful for grilled meats and fish.

INGREDIENTS

12 lamb cutlets, trimmed
4 ripe plum tomatoes, chopped
salt and freshly ground
　black pepper
1 tbsp balsamic vinegar

For the marinade

1 red onion, finely chopped
2 garlic cloves, crushed

1 tsp ground cumin
¼ tsp smoked paprika
1 tsp ground coriander
grated zest and juice of 1 lemon
6 tbsp olive oil, plus extra
　for drizzling
handful of mint, roughly chopped
handful of coriander, chopped

METHOD

1 Place the trimmed cutlets in a dish. In a mixing bowl, combine the red onion, garlic, cumin, paprika, ground coriander, lemon juice and zest, olive oil, and most of the chopped mint and coriander to make the marinade. Rub the marinade over the lamb and leave to marinate for at least 30 minutes.

2 Season the chopped tomatoes with salt and pepper, drizzle with the balsamic vinegar, a little olive oil, and the remaining coriander and mint. Set aside.

3 Preheat the grill on its highest setting. Remove the cutlets from the marinade and grill for 5 minutes each side, or until cooked and crisp. Serve the lamb with the tomato salad alongside.

serves 6

prep 15 mins
plus marinating
• cook 10 mins

GUIDELINES per serving

GI

calories

saturated fat

salt

Pork and apple patties

Miniature burgers made from a few simple ingredients.

INGREDIENTS

450g minced pork
2 crisp eating apples, cored
  and finely diced
salt and freshly ground black pepper
1 egg
1 tsp paprika
4–5 stalks of fresh thyme,
  leaves only, finely chopped
oil for frying

METHOD

1 Place the pork in a bowl with the apple, season well with salt and black pepper, and mix together. Add the egg, paprika, and thyme and mix until combined, then, using your hands, squeeze the mixture together until it is an even paste. Shape into 8 balls (2 per serving) and pat into patties.

2 Heat the oil in a large non-stick frying pan and add the patties, working in batches if necessary. Cook over a medium heat for 3–4 minutes each side, until a deep golden colour. Transfer to a plate lined with kitchen paper to drain, then serve.

serves 4
makes 8

prep 15 mins
• cook 10 mins

1 month
after step 1

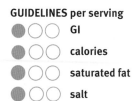

GUIDELINES per serving
GI
calories
saturated fat
salt

Ragout of venison with wild mushrooms

This slowly simmered stew concentrates all the rich flavours of the venison and mushrooms.

INGREDIENTS

1 tbsp olive oil
15g (½oz) butter
4 shallots, sliced
115g (4oz) smoked bacon, diced
600g (1lb 5oz) venison, diced
1 tbsp plain flour
3 tbsp brandy

250g (9oz) wild mushrooms, sliced
250ml (9fl oz) beef stock
1 tbsp tomato purée
1 tbsp Worcestershire sauce
1 tsp dried oregano
salt and freshly ground black pepper

METHOD

1 Heat the oil and butter in a large flameproof casserole and fry the shallots and bacon over a medium-high heat, stirring frequently, until beginning to brown.

2 Add the venison and fry for 3–4 minutes, or until browned on all sides, stirring frequently. Stir in the flour, then cook for 1–2 minutes, or until beginning to brown. Add the brandy and stir for 30 seconds, then add the mushrooms and stock. Bring to the boil, stirring often.

3 Stir in the tomato purée, Worcestershire sauce, and oregano, and season to taste with salt and pepper. Reduce the heat to low, cover tightly with a lid, and simmer very gently for 1½–2 hours, or until the venison is tender (the cooking time will depend on the age of the meat). Serve hot, straight from the casserole.

serves 4

prep 15 mins
• cook 1 ¾-2 ¼ hours

3 month

GUIDELINES per serving
GI
calories
saturated fat
salt

Dark chocolate and yogurt ice cream

Rich in taste but lower in calories than ordinary ice cream.

INGREDIENTS
300ml (10fl oz) milk
200g (7oz) dark chocolate
 (at least 70% cocoa solids),
 broken into small pieces
calorie-free sweetener
4 egg yolks
250ml (8fl oz) low-fat natural yogurt

METHOD
1 Put the milk, chocolate, and calorie-free sweetener to taste in a small pan and heat gently, stirring occasionally, until the chocolate has melted. Bring the mixture just to the boil, then remove from the heat.
2 Whisk the egg yolks together, then slowly pour into the chocolate mixture and whisk until the mixture is smooth.
3 Leave to cool for 15 minutes, then whisk in the yogurt and spoon into a freezer-proof container. Cover with a lid and leave to cool completely, then transfer to the freezer to freeze overnight.

serves 6

prep 25 mins
• cook 2 mins

GUIDELINES per serving
GI
calories
saturated fat
salt

Poached pears with toasted almonds

A classic, elegant dessert that can be made with such ease: treat yourself.

INGREDIENTS
juice of 4 oranges
zest of 1 orange
1 cinnamon stick
2 star anise
4 just-ripe pears, halved lengthways
   and cored
50g (1¾oz) blanched almonds
250g (9oz) reduced-fat Greek-style
   yogurt, to serve

METHOD
1 Put the orange juice and zest in a pan along with 200ml (7fl oz) water, the cinnamon stick, and star anise. Bring to the boil.
2 Reduce to a simmer and add the pears. Cover with a lid and cook for 10–15 minutes, or until the pears are soft and tender. Remove with a slotted spoon and put on a serving plate or plates. Bring the juice to the boil and spoon a little over the pears.
3 Meanwhile, put the almonds in a small frying pan and toast them for a few minutes until golden, stirring occasionally so that they don't burn. Serve the pears topped with the almonds and a spoonful of Greek yogurt.

serves 4

prep 10 mins
• cook 20 mins

GUIDELINES per serving

GI

calories

saturated fat

salt

Apricot crumble

By cooking apricots with a little orange, it helps to bring out their flavour and make this a truly moreish crumble.

INGREDIENTS

700g (1lb 9oz) apricots, stoned
  and cut into quarters
juice and zest of 1 large orange
2–3 tbsp sucralose sweetener
  (Splenda)
60g (2oz) plain white flour
60g (2oz) plain wholemeal flour
60g (2oz) jumbo oats
85g (3oz) polyunsaturated margarine
60g (2oz) fructose

METHOD

1 Preheat the oven to 180°C (350°F/Gas 4). Place the apricots and the orange juice and zest in a saucepan and cook over a gentle heat until the apricots are soft. Stir in the sweetener and taste to check the sweetness. Set aside.
2 To make the crumble topping, mix together both types of flour and the oats. Rub in the margarine until the mixture resembles coarse breadcrumbs. Stir in the fructose.
3 Spoon the apricots into a shallow heatproof dish, sprinkle the crumble topping over them evenly, and bake for 20 minutes, or until the topping is golden brown.

serves 4

prep 10 mins
• cook 20 mins

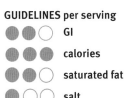

GUIDELINES per serving

GI

calories

saturated fat

salt

Lemon cheesecake

This low-fat version of a traditional baked cheesecake is just as full of creamy flavour.

INGREDIENTS

100g (3½oz) sucralose
  sweetener (Splenda)
juice of 2 lemons and zest of 3 lemons
4 eggs, separated
150g (5½oz) low-fat cream cheese
200g (7oz) quark cheese
50g (1¾oz) sultanas
2 tbsp plain flour
butter for greasing

METHOD

1 Preheat the oven to 170°C (340°F/Gas 3½). In a large bowl, dissolve the sweetener in the lemon juice, then add the egg yolks and whisk until pale and thick. Add the cream cheese and quark and beat until smooth and well combined.

2 Add the lemon zest and sultanas to the cream cheese mixture, and stir to mix. Sprinkle the flour over the mixture and fold it in gently. In a clean bowl, using a clean whisk, whisk the egg whites until stiff, then fold into the cheese mixture.

3 Spoon the mixture into a deep, round, 20cm (8in) springform cake tin, greased and lined with greaseproof paper. Bake in the oven for 45–50 minutes or until golden and almost set; it should still wobble slightly in the centre. Leave to cool in the oven with the door open (this should prevent it from cracking too much).

4 Once cooled, run a knife around the edge of tin, release the sides and carefully remove the cheesecake.

 serves 8

 prep 5 mins
• cook 50 mins

GUIDELINES per serving
◐○○ GI
●○○ calories
◑○○ saturated fat
●○○ salt

Banana and pecan muffins

The banana helps sweeten the muffin mixture, reducing the need for sugar in the recipe.

INGREDIENTS

125g (4½oz) wholemeal flour
3 tbsp caster sugar
2 tsp baking powder
85g (3oz) pecan nuts,
  roughly chopped
generous pinch of ground cinnamon
1 egg, beaten
4 tbsp semi-skimmed milk
4 tbsp sunflower oil
2 ripe bananas (about 225g/8oz),
  roughly mashed

METHOD

1 Preheat the oven to 200°C (400°F/Gas 6). Place the flour, sugar, baking powder, pecan nuts, and ground cinnamon in a bowl. Mix them together and make a well in the centre.
2 In a separate bowl, mix together the egg, milk, and oil. Pour the mixture into the dry ingredients and stir until just blended. Stir in the bananas, taking care not to over-mix.
3 Fill the paper cases in the muffin tray two-thirds full, then place the tray in the oven and bake for 20–25 minutes, or until a skewer inserted into the centre comes out clean.
4 Transfer the muffins to a wire rack to cool. Store in an airtight container; the muffins will keep for up to three days.

 makes 6

 prep 10 mins
• cook 20-25 mins

 3 months

 6 hole muffin tray lined with 6 paper cases

GUIDELINES per serving

●●○ GI
●●○ calories
●○○ saturated fat
●○○ salt

Senior Editor Cécile Landau

Designer Elma Aquino

Jacket Designer Mark Penfound

Special Sales Creative Project Manager Alison Donovan

Pre-Production Producer Rob Dunn

Producer Igrain Roberts

DK INDIA

Editorial Consultant Dipali Singh

Designer Neha Ahuja

DTP Designer Tarun Sharma

DTP Coordinator Sunil Sharma

Head of Publishing Aparna Sharma

This paperback edition published in 2017
First published in Great Britain in 2013
Material previously published in
The Diabetes Cooking Book (2010) by Dorling Kindersley
Limited , 80 Strand, London WC2R 0RL

Copyright © 2010, 2013, 2017 Dorling Kindersley

2 4 6 8 10 9 7 5 3 1
001–192537–Nov/2017

A CIP catalogue record for this book is available
from the British Library.

ISBN 978-0-2413-1820-1

Printed and bound in China

A WORLD OF IDEAS
SEE ALL THERE IS TO KNOW

www.dk.com